VIS COMICA*

The power to make people laugh: from an epigram by Caesar on Terence, the Latin poet.

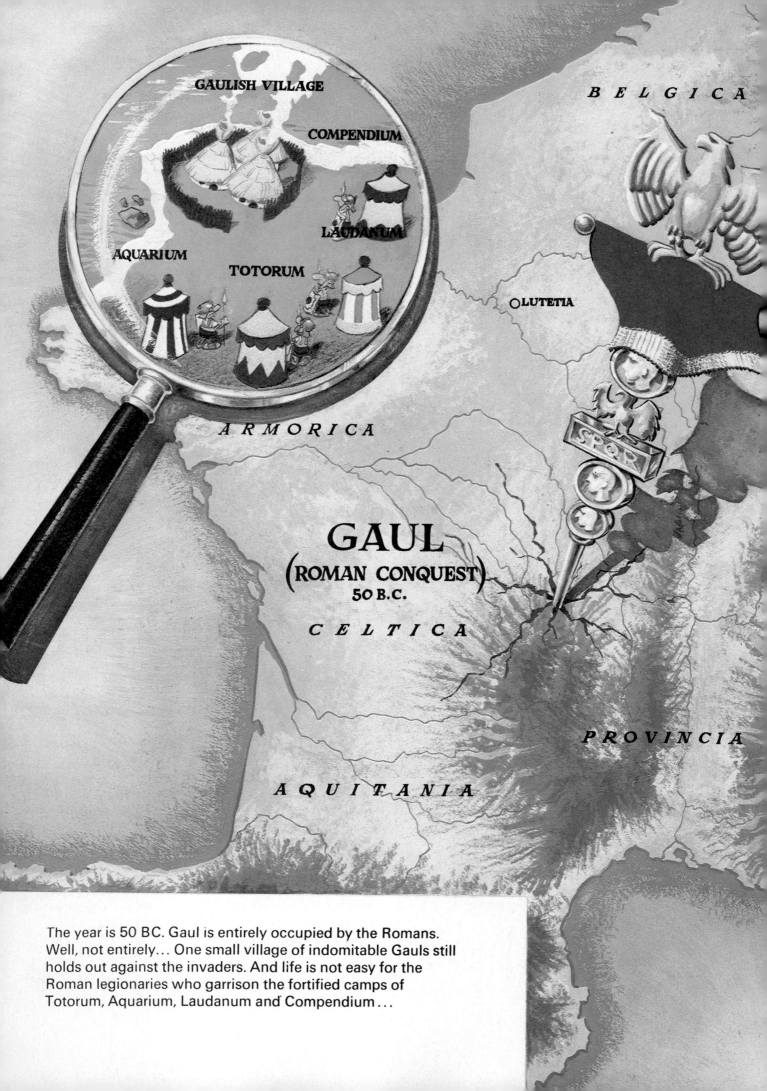

The year is 50 BC. Gaul is entirely occupied by the Romans. Well, not entirely... One small village of indomitable Gauls still holds out against the invaders. And life is not easy for the Roman legionaries who garrison the fortified camps of Totorum, Aquarium, Laudanum and Compendium...

COME ALONG, CHILDREN! BREAK'S OVER!

BONG! BONG! BONG!

WE'VE DECIDED TO REMOVE OUR CHILDREN FROM THIS SCHOOL! IT HAS A POOR REPUTATION!

?!?

WHAT'S MORE, WE'VE APPOINTED A NEW TEACHER FROM LUTETIA! SHE'S GOING TO SEE TO THEIR EDUCATION!

SPECIALLY THEIR *MUSICAL* EDUCATION!

!

ALLOW ME TO REMIND YOU THAT ONLY DRUIDS AND BARDS ARE QUALIFIED TO TEACH SCHOOLCHILDREN!

OH, SO A WOMAN CAN'T BE A BARD?

NO, MA'AM! SHE'S BARRED FROM BEING A BARD!!!

THAT'S JUST TOO BARD! TAKE THAT!

KEEP YOUR HANDS TO YOURSELF, MA'AM!

PAFF!

NO HOLDS BARRED, EH?

NOT ONLY DO THEY THUMP ME AT THE DROP OF A LYRE, THEY'RE BRINGING IN A FOREIGN FEMALE TO REPLACE ME! WELL, THAT'S IT! I'M LEAVING THE VILLAGE!

POOR OLD CACOFONIX! HE REALLY SEEMS TO MEAN IT! I'D BETTER GO AND TELL CHIEF VITALSTATISTIX!

IT'S NO SKIN OFF MY NOSE! NO WOMAN COULD EVER REPLACE ME! CARVING MENHIRS IS FAR TOO DELICATE A JOB!

CHIEF VITALSTATISTIX! CACOFONIX IS PLANNING TO LEAVE US OVER A WOMAN BARD!

YOU MEAN HE'S IN LOVE?

NO, BUT HE'S ALL UPSET TO THINK HE'S BEING REPLACED BY A WOMAN FROM OUT-SIDE THE VILLAGE!

OH, I HAVE EVERY FAITH IN US! WE'LL SEE THIS WOMAN BARD OFF IN DOUBLE-QUICK TIME!

MEANWHILE WE MUST PERSUADE CACOFONIX TO STAY. HE'S EXCELLENT COMPANY WHEN HE DOESN'T SING!

THE WHOLE VILLAGE ASKS YOU NOT TO LEAVE, CACOFONIX!

FAREWELL, YOU UNGRATEFUL LOT! QUALIS ARTIFEX PEREO!*

*WHAT AN ARTIST PERISHES WITH ME! (LATIN SAYING WRONGLY ATTRIBUTED TO NERO)

3A

LOOK...JUST TO SHOW HOW FOND WE ARE OF YOU, WE'RE EVEN WILLING TO... TO LET YOU SING!

OH NO, YOU WON'T GET ME TO SING! OH NO, YOU WON'T GET ME TO SING!!!

WHERE ARE YOU GOING, CACOFONIX?

I AM RETIRING TO MY LITTLE PIED-A-L'AIR* IN THE HEART OF THE FOREST TO MEDITATE ON MAN'S INGRATITUDE!

* A BARD'S SECOND HOME.

IT'S SAD TO SEE OUR BARD LEAVE THE VILLAGE!

YES, THOUGH IT'S NOT ALWAYS THE BEST WHO ARE TAKEN!

IS THIS THE VILLAGE OF LOONIES?

!?

3B

LOOKS LIKE IT'S NOT ALWAYS THE BEST WHO REPLACE THEM, EITHER!

PFFFFFF!

SSSH!

MADAM, I AM THE CHIEFTAIN OF THIS VILLAGE! KINDLY MODERATE YOUR LANGUAGE!

SORRY, BUT THAT'S HOW THEY'VE BEEN DESCRIBING YOUR OPPIDUM IN EVERY MANSIO* WHERE I ASKED THE WAY SINCE LUTETIA!

*KIND OF MOTEL ON THE ROMAN ROADS.

PFFFFFHEE! HEEHEE!

SO YOU'RE THE... WHAT DO WE CALL YOU? BARDESS? BARDETTE?

JUST BARD! MY NAME IS BRAVURA, AND TELL YOUR HYSTERICAL FRIEND TO STOP THAT SILLY GIGGLING OR I SHALL LOSE MY TEMPER!

SHUT UP, OBELIX!

HOHOHAHAHA!

ER...PLEASE FORGIVE MY FRIEND! HE'S NEVER SEEN A WOMAN WEARING THE BREECHES BEFORE!

YOU IGNORANT RUSTICS! ORIENTAL 'DJEANS', LEVIX AND LEGGINGS LIKE THESE ARE ALL THE RAGE IN LUTETIA!

SRRR!

IT ISN'T THAT... TEEHEEHEE! EVERYONE KNOWS IT'S VERTICAL STRIPES THAT ARE SLIMMING... HO! HO! HO!

!

RIGHT, FATSO, LET'S SEE IF YOU'RE AS STRONG ON MATHEMATICS AS AESTHETICS! SAY YOUR III TIMES TABLE!

EASY! ONE TIMES THREE IS ASTERIX, DOGMATIX AND ME, BUT THREE TIMES BOARS MAKES A LOT MORE ON THE TABLE, OF COURSE!

RIGHT. I WANT TO SEE YOU AND YOUR STRIPES IN MY CLASS TOMORROW, GET IT?

?!

BONG! BONG! BONG!

BUT I CAN'T! NOT TOMORROW! I'VE GOT MENHIRS TO DELIVER!

OBELIX, PLEASE! DON'T COMPLICATE MATTERS!

PFFFFFF TEEHEEHEE!

8

WE'VE BEEN LOOKING FORWARD TO SEEING YOU, MA'AM! I'M IMPEDIMENTA, THE CHIEF'S WIFE. MEET MRS UNHYGIENIX, MRS FULLIAUTOMATIX AND MRS GERIATRIX.

JUST CALL ME BRAVURA!

WE'RE HAVING A LITTLE PARTY IN YOUR HONOUR THIS EVENING, TO INTRODUCE OUR NEW BARD TO THE VILLAGERS.

YOU MAY FIND THEM A BIT RUSTIC, BUT THEY'RE FULL OF FUN!

SO I'VE SEEN! WELL, WHERE'S MY OFFICIAL RESIDENCE?

YOUR OFFICIAL RES... OH, YES, OF COURSE!

WHY NOT USE CACOFONIX'S HUT? HE LEFT...HE DIDN'T KNOW THE SCORE.

YES, HE GOT THE WIND UP!

SO IT'S YOURS!

NO STRINGS ATTACHED! COME ALONG...YOU MUST BE WORN OUT, WALKING ALL THIS WAY!

I DON'T HITCH LIFTS. YOU NEVER KNOW WHAT MALE CHAUVINIST PIG YOU MAY MEET!

OINK?

54

THERE! RATHER HIGH UP, BUT THE AIR IS VERY PURE!

HUMPH! NOT BAD!

SOON AFTER-WARDS...

YOU KNOW ME, ASTERIX: I'M NOT A MISOGYNIST, I'M NOT XENO?HOBIC, BUT I DON'T LIKE THAT FOREIGN WOMAN. SOMETHING TELLS ME SHE'S GOING TO BRING THE SKY DOWN ON OUR HEADS!

IT'S A LONG TIME SINCE ANYONE SWEPT UP AROUND HERE!

?!

WHAT DID I TELL YOU?

I KNEW CACOFONIX DIDN'T COMPOSE LIGHT MUSIC, BUT I HAD NO IDEA HE WAS A MAN OF SO MUCH NOTE!

TING!

5B

9

A PARTY IN HONOUR OF THAT ...THAT BARD! *HUMPH!* HONESTLY!

OH, I SEE! JUST FOR ONCE WE WELCOME A PERSON OF QUALITY AND EDUCATION TO THE VILLAGE, AND MISTER VITALSTATISTIX DOESN'T LIKE IT!

I DARE SAY HE'D PREFER THE BORING COMPANY OF THOSE COARSE, UNCULTIVATED BOORS WHO CHOSE HIM AS CHIEF!

LISTEN, 'PEDIMENTA DEAR...

AND STOP CALLING ME 'PEDIMENTA! IT'S COMMON! AND RIDICULOUS!

WHERE'S YOUR SHIELD OF OFFICE?

ONE OF MY SHIELD-BEARERS HAS LET ME DOWN, TIRED OUT, AND THE OTHER FLATLY REFUSES TO CARRY ME ALONE!

I THINK I NEED A SPARE SHIELD-BEARER!

YOU DO. THAT SHIELD IS ALWAYS BREAKING DOWN AT THE CRUCIAL MOMENT.

6A

I DIDN'T THINK THERE COULD BE WOMEN BARDS!

WE ARE ENTERING THE MODERN ERA OF THE ANCIENT WORLD, ASTERIX, WHEN ANYTHING MAY HAPPEN!

SO IT'S ONLY RIGHT FOR A WOMAN TO BE CONSIDERED THE EQUAL OF A MAN, WITH ALL THE ASPIRATIONS AND AMBITIONS HITHERTO DENIED HER!

YOU MEAN THERE COULD BE WOMEN DRUIDS TOO?

OH, COME ON, ASTERIX, BE SERIOUS!

DO TELL US ABOUT GAY LUTETIA, DEAR BRAVURA! I HEAR IT'S BECOMING A GREAT CITY!

YES, IT'S REALLY CAPITAL!

WHAT ARE THE SUMMER FASHIONS THIS YEAR?

DO YOU THINK ORIENTAL DJEANS OR LEGGINGS WOULD FLATTER MY FIGURE?

WELCOME TO OUR NEW B

6B

*GAULISH TRUMPET

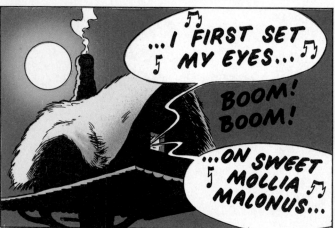

12

NEXT DAY...

OUR NEW BARD LOOKS CROTCHETY THIS MORNING!

YEAH, SHE FELL FLAT!

BONG! BONG! BONG!

GET IN LINE, AND NO TALKING, PLEASE!

SCHOOL

I'M OFF TO HUNT WILD BOAR! I'LL LEAVE YOU TO YOUR LESSONS, OBELIX!

ANIMALS ARE FORBIDDEN IN SCHOOL!

BUT DOGMATIX ISN'T TOO OLD A DOG TO LEARN A FEW NEW TRICKS!

I SAID ANIMALS ARE FORBIDDEN IN SCHOOL!

THERE, NOW YOU'VE GONE AND UPSET HIM!

GRRRRR!

NEVER MIND, DOGMATIX! WAIT FOR ME HERE. I'LL TELL YOU ALL ABOUT IT!

AND WHAT, MAY I ASK, IS THAT?

MY LUNCH-BUNDLE! THAT'S NOT FORBIDDEN, I HOPE?

SOON AFTERWARDS...

RIGHT, WE'RE GOING TO SAY OUR V TIMES TABLE! ALL TOGETHER NOW!

I TIMES V IS V, II TIMES V IS X, III TIMES...

MISS! PLEASE, MISS, OBELIX IS TRYING TO GET AT MY LUNCH-BUNDLE!

I WAS ONLY GOING TO HAVE A TASTE, THAT'S ALL!

RIGHT, YOU WILL CARVE OUT 100 TIMES: I MUST NOT GET AT SOMEONE ELSE'S LUNCH-BUNDLE!

13

AT THIS VERY MOMENT, IN ROME...

WELL, MANLIUS CLAPHAMOMNIBUS, HOW ARE YOU DOING WITH THAT 'VERY SPECIAL CENTURY' YOU WERE GOING TO RECRUIT?

IT'S READY TO GO, O CAESAR! YOUR NEW SECRET WEAPON MERELY AWAITS YOUR ORDERS TO EMBARK!

I DON'T WANT ANY WITNESSES TO THIS BUSINESS, UNDERSTAND? NO WITNESSES!

EVERY PRECAUTION SHALL BE TAKEN, O CAESAR, I SWEAR IT!

IF THE EXISTENCE OF YOUR CENTURY BECAME KNOWN, I SHOULD BE VULNERABLE TO MY ENEMIES IN THE SENATE AND THE LAUGHING-STOCK OF ROME! SO WATCH IT, CLAPHAMOMNIBUS!

GULP!

AND THUS A ROMAN SHIP, CARRYING CAESAR'S MYSTERIOUS SECRET WEAPON, SETS SAIL IN THE DIRECTION OF... GAUL!

POOR OBELIX! WHAT A PITY HE COULDN'T COME ON THIS HUNT...

... HE'D HAVE HAD SUCH FUN!

GLUG! GLUG! GLUG!

A LITTLE LATER, IN THE FORTIFIED CAMP OF AQUARIUM...

BY JUPITER! ANYONE WOULD THINK ALL GAUL HAD BEEN TRAMPLING OVER YOU!

IT FEELF LIKE IT, FENTURION!

WE BUMPED INTO A BOAR...

...AND THAT LITTLE STINKER FROM THE VILLAGE OF INDOMITABLE GAULS!

GLORIA VICTIS!

BEAR UP, BOYS! ROME HAS PROMISED TO SEND OUR RELIEF SOON!

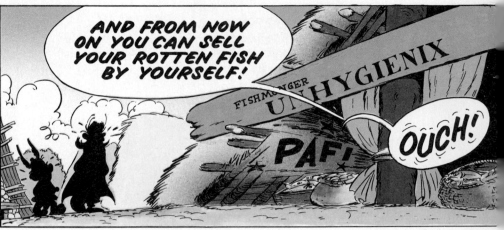

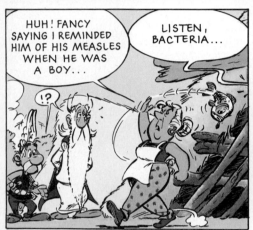

THE VILLAGE COUNCIL MEETS...

WE MUST GO AND TELL THAT BARD SHE'S REDUNDANT BEFORE THINGS GET ANY WORSE. SHE MUST LEAVE THE VILLAGE.

I CAN THINK OF ONLY ONE WARRIOR PROUD AND BRAVE ENOUGH TO BREAK THAT NEWS!

WHO?

YOU, ASTERIX!

OH NO! WHY DOES IT HAVE TO BE ME? I'M NO PROUDER OR BRAVER THAN THE NEXT MAN, AND I'M REALLY NOT CUT OUT FOR THIS SORT OF...

ASTERIX, PLEASE! DON'T COMPLICATE MATTERS!

...MISSION!

PFFFFFFFF!

PFFFFFFFF!

BE FIRM AND UNYIELDING, ASTERIX!

WHERE ARE YOU GOING, ASTERIX?

GUESS!

WHY DID IT HAVE TO BE ME? I MEAN, I'M A BACHELOR! NONE OF THIS HAS ANYTHING TO DO WITH ME!

SOMETIMES I REALLY ENVY CACOFONIX, LIVING IN THE DEPTHS OF THE FOREST! (SIGH...)

MA'AM... ER... I'VE BEEN SENT TO TELL YOU THAT...

AH, YOU'RE THE LITTLE FELLOW WHO ISN'T AFRAID OF THE BIG BOYS?

SLAP!

YOU KNOW, I LIKE YOU! I WANTED A WORD WITH YOU MYSELF!

SCHOOL

TONIGHT GAULISH WOMEN'S MOVEMENT WORKSHOP

20

WHAT ARE YOU DOING, VITALSTATISTIX?

I'M THE VICTIM OF A *COUP D'ÉTAT* LED BY THAT ✦✦✦! LUTETIAN WOMAN! I'M GOING INTO POLITICAL EXILE!

WHERE?

IN THE FOREST, WITH CACOFONIX!

QUICK! WE MUST WARN GETAFIX THE DRUID!

! !

LONG LIVE CHIEF IMPEDIMENTA!

HEY! YOU WITH THE WIDE STRIPES! FATSO!

WHAT FATSO? WHAT WIDE STRIPES?

EVERYONE'S TALENTS MUST BE FULLY UTILIZED! IN FUTURE YOU WILL GO HUNTING AND COOK OUR NEW CHIEF'S MEALS!

ASTERIX, I HAVE THIS TERRIBLE URGE TO THUMP SOMEONE!

KEEP CALM, OBELIX! LET'S GO AND SEE GETAFIX!

VITALSTATISTIX IS LEAVING TOO. THIS BRAVURA IS REALLY DANGEROUS, GETAFIX!

TRUE, BUT THE VILLAGERS ARE FREE TO CHOOSE, ASTERIX! IF THEY'VE DECIDED THEY WANT IMPEDIMENTA AS THEIR CHIEF, WE MUST ACCEPT IT!

MY STRIPES AREN'T THAT WIDE, ANYWAY!

I'M SURE IT WAS ONLY A MINORITY DECISION! WE MUST ORGANIZE A REFERENDUM!

WE'RE GOING TO TAKE A FREE VOTE ON WHETHER IMPEDIMENTA OR VITALSTATISTIX IS TO BE OUR CHIEF!

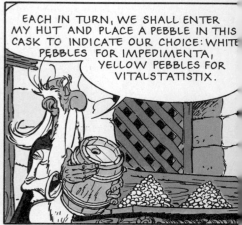

EACH IN TURN, WE SHALL ENTER MY HUT AND PLACE A PEBBLE IN THIS CASK TO INDICATE OUR CHOICE: WHITE PEBBLES FOR IMPEDIMENTA, YELLOW PEBBLES FOR VITALSTATISTIX.

OH, WHY MAKE IT SO COMPLICATED WHEN A SIMPLE SHOW OF HANDS WOULD DO?

SHE'S RIGHT! LET'S HAVE A SHOW OF HANDS!

HUH! WHY NOT A SHOW OF FEET WHILE WE'RE ABOUT IT?

OH YES, YOU'D GET A BIG KICK OUT OF THAT!

NOT EXACTLY UNANIMOUS, ARE THEY?

IT'S PERFECTLY SIMPLE! LET'S VOTE BY A SHOW OF HANDS TO SHOW IF WE WANT TO VOTE BY A SHOW OF HANDS!

ALL WHO WANT TO VOTE BY A SHOW OF HANDS SHOW THEIR HANDS!

RIGHT. ALL WHO DON'T WANT TO VOTE BY A SHOW OF HANDS SHOW THEIR HANDS!

ASTERIX, I DON'T QUITE UNDERSTAND THIS SHOW OF HANDS BUSINESS!

I DO! I CALL IT A POOR SHOW, AND I'M THROWING IN MY HAND!

NOW THEN, MY PROUD LITTLE GAUL, DON'T BE CROSS! I'M SURE WE CAN SETTLE THIS AMICABLY!

YOU LEAVE ME ALONE!

LISTEN, DID YOU EVER THINK OF SETTLING DOWN?

MIND YOUR OWN BUSINESS!

BECAUSE IF SO, I WOULDN'T MIND SETTLING DOWN WITH YOU MYSELF!

WH... WHAT?

WE COULD DO GREAT THINGS TOGETHER! FOR INSTANCE, WE COULD BECOME CHIEFS OF THIS VILLAGE!

OH YES?

SO THAT'S YOUR LITTLE GAME! YOU HAVE DESIGNS ON THE CHIEFTAIN'S SHIELD!!!

WHY, MY PROUD LITTLE GAUL LOOKS EVEN MORE HANDSOME WHEN HE'S ANGRY!

STOP THIS CRAZY TALK, OR I'LL...

SMACK!

TCHAC!

OH, BY ALL THE GODS! WHAT HAVE I DONE? I'VE STRUCK A WOMAN! I CAN'T BELIEVE IT... IT'S NOT LIKE ME AT ALL!

I'M...ER...I'M TERRIBLY SORRY! I DIDN'T MEAN TO...

I DO APOLOGIZE! IT'S THE FIRST TIME I EVER...

IN FUTURE I'M STEERING CLEAR OF UNSCRUPULOUS AND SHAMELESS MIDGETS!

PERHAPS WE SHOULDN'T HAVE BEEN SO HARD ON ASTERIX!

WE'VE UPSET OUR DRUID!

SUPPOSE THE ROMANS ATTACK?

HOWEVER SHALL WE MANAGE WITHOUT MAGIC POTION?

HAVE NO FEAR! THE ROMANS WILL NOT REFUSE THE PEACE I'M GOING TO OFFER THEM!

'OON AFTER-VARDS...

WE'RE LETTING BRAVURA OFF LIGHTLY, LEAVING THE VILLAGE!

OF COURSE, BUT WE'LL KEEP A CLOSE WATCH ON DEVELOP-MENTS!

HEY! WAIT FOR US!

YOU REALLY THINK A MENHIR IS A NECESSITY OF LIFE IN THE FOREST?

IT'S FOR DOGMATIX...

HE DOES LOVE TREES, BUT THERE ARE TIMES WHEN HE PREFERS A NICE MENHIR!

YOU KNOW, I'M SURPRISED BY THE APATHY AND INDIFFER-ENCE OF THE MEN OF THE VILLAGE!

FISHMONGER YGIENIX

CLOSED

PUT YOURSELF IN THEIR PLACE! THEY HAVE FAMILY TIES YOU AND I DON'T HAVE, ASTERIX!

TOMATIX

CLOSED

!?

ONE AGAINST ALL AND ALL FOR ONE!

YOU GO HOME, SON!

IT'TH ALWAYTH THE THAME! THE GROWN-UPTH GET ALL THE FUN!

BOC!

MEANWHILE, ON THE COAST NEAR THE FORTIFIED CAMP OF AQUARIUM...

STAND BY TO DISEMBARK!

CREEEEAK!

OH FOR SOME NICE SEA AIR!

I'LL ASK YOU TO BE PATIENT A LITTLE LONGER DON'T COME OUT BEFORE I GIVE THE ORDER!

AND IN THE FORTIFIED CAMP OF AQUARIUM...

SNIFF! THE GAULS HAB GOT A FORBIDABLE ABD DABGEROUS WEAPOB...

...THEIR WRETCHEB BARB WHO CAB OBLY SING SO BADLY...

...THAT HE BRINGS DOWB THE CURSE OF THE GOBS WHEBEVER HE SINGS!

?!

BLOW!

QUOB ERAT BEMONSTRAN-BAAA... TISHOOO!

IT'LL BE A GREAT RELIEF WHEN THE RELIEF GETS HERE!

THE RELIEF'S HERE, CENTURION!

ARE...ARE YOU THE RELIEF?

SO TO SPEAK! MY ORDERS FROM CAESAR ARE TO TELL YOU TO LEAVE CAMP BEFORE THE RELIEF RELIEVES YOU!

AND SUPPOSE I REFUSE TO LEAVE CAMP BEFORE THE RELIEF RELIEVES US?

THEN YOU'LL BE RELIEVED OF YOUR DUTIES AND GO TO RELIEVE THE MONOTONY OF THE DIET OF THE LIONS IN THE CIRCUS!

WE'RE LEAVING CAMP!

MEANWHILE, IN THE FOREST SEPARATING THE VILLAGE FROM THE ROMAN CAMP...

WE'RE NOT TOO BADLY OFF HERE WHILE WE WAIT FOR OUR GOOD LADIES TO SEE SENSE!

BUT WE MUST BE ON OUR GUARD, IN CASE THE ROMANS TAKE THEIR CHANCE TO SEIZE THE VILLAGE!

OBELIX AND I WILL GO AND KEEP WATCH ON THEM!

26

28

STOP IT! STOP IT AT ONCE!

PIF!

PAF!

A FINE PERFORMANCE BY THE ROMAN ARMY, EH? YOU DON'T EVEN NEED GAULS TO FIGHT NOW! HOW THEY'D LAUGH IF THEY COULD SEE YOU!

I DON'T SEE ANYTHING TO LAUGH ABOUT!

SSH, OBELIX!

I THOUGHT I TOLD YOU TO LEAVE CAMP, CENTURION!

LISTEN, WHAT EXACTLY IS THE IDEA?

COME HERE A MINUTE! I HAVE SOMETHING TO TELL YOU!

?

25A

I GOT THE IDEA OF RECRUITING THIS CENTURY OF WOMEN TO CONQUER THE GAULS AND OCCUPY THEIR VILLAGE AT LONG LAST!

YOU THINK YOUR SECRET WEAPON WILL SUCCEED WHERE WE'VE FAILED, DO YOU?

?!?

THEIR FAMOUS GAULISH GALLANTRY WILL PREVENT THE INDOMITABLE VILLAGERS FROM FIGHTING WOMEN, EVEN WOMEN IN UNIFORM!

I GET IT! RIGHT, WE'LL LEAVE CAMP!

OH NO, YOU WON'T! NOW YOU KNOW THE SECRET YOU'RE ALL CONFINED TO BARRACKS!

?!?

QUICK! WE MUST GO AND WARN OUR CHIEF!

ASTERIX, WHAT'S GAULISH GALLANTRY?

25B

IF WE FIGHT THOSE WOMEN LEGIONARIES WE SHALL BE DISHONOURED, AND IF WE DON'T THEY'LL OCCUPY OUR VILLAGE!

BY TOUTATIS! WE MUST WARN OUR GOOD LADIES OF THE DANGER THREATENING THEM!

WE'RE THE VICTIMS OF OUR OWN REPUTATION!

A VOLUNTEER TO GO TO THE VILLAGE!

ME, GO BACK TO THE VILLAGE? NEVER!

MY WIFE MIGHT THINK I'D BEEN LOOKING FOR SOME EXCUSE TO GO BACK!

I CAN JUST SEE ALL THOSE DISHES WAITING FOR ME!

NOT ME! NOTHING DOING!

ONE HAS ONE'S PRIDE!

OKAY, I GET THE IDEA! COME ON, OBELIX!

26

YOU DON'T LOOK HAPPY, OBELIX.

I'M BORED, ASTERIX! CACOFONIX IS PUTTING ALL THE FOREST BOARS TO FLIGHT...

...AND WE AREN'T EVEN ALLOWED TO THUMP ROMANS NOW THEY'RE ROMAN MATRONS! THESE MATRONS ARE CRAZY!

BY TOUTATIS! THE VILLAGE LOOKS DESERTED!

IT'S THE CACOFONIX EFFECT! BRAVURA'S PUTTING EVERYONE TO FLIGHT! THESE BARDS ARE CRAZY!

UNHYGIENIX

26

BY TOUTATITH, THETHE ROMANTH ARE CRATHY!

HERE, SONNY! WHERE ARE ALL THE VILLAGE WOMEN?

CLING! CLANG!

THEY'RE ALL AT THCOOL! UTH CHILDREN AREN'T HAVING LETHONTH ANY MORE! IT'TH GREAT!

?

LET'S TAKE A LOOK, OBELIX!

SCHOOL

CLAP! CLAP! CLAP!

BRAVO!

AND STILL IN THE *DIORIX* COLLECTION, AFTER THE MENHIR ROSE OUTFIT, WE PRESENT THE DREAMY DOLMEN EVENING DRESS!

CLAP! CLAP! CLAP! CLAP! CLAP! CLAP! CLAP! CLAP! CLAP!

THIS IS REALLY WEIRD!

SNIFF! SNIFF! SNIFF! YOU'RE RIGHT... I CAN'T SMELL UN-HYGIENIX'S UNFRESH FISH ANY MORE!

CLAP! CLAP! CLAP!

HEY... WHAT'S GOING ON?

BRAVURA HAS BROUGHT SOME FAMOUS FASHION DESIGNERS FROM LUTETIA TO PRESENT THEIR SPRING COLLECTIONS!

CLAP! CLAP! CLAP!

IT'S... *IT'S ASTERIX!*

WHERE ARE OUR HUSBANDS?

WHAT ARE THEY DOING?

HOW ARE THEY?

WHEN ARE THEY COMING HOME?

!?

HUH! SLAVES YOU WERE AND SLAVES YOU WILL REMAIN!

QUIET, PLEASE! MOVE BACK! ASTERIX MAY HAVE SOMETHING TO TELL US.

I'M SORRY TO INTERRUPT THE SHOW, BUT VITALSTATISTIX HAS SENT ME TO TELL YOU THAT...

THE COUNCIL WILL MEET IN MY HUT TO HEAR WHAT THAT GREAT BOOR HAS TO TELL US!

SOON AFTERWARDS...

SO CAESAR HAS DISCOVERED THE WEAKNESS OF THE GAULS!

FACING THOSE WOMEN LEGIONARIES, WE MEN ARE HELPLESS!

I KNOW SOMEONE WHO WASN'T ALWAYS SO SCRUPULOUS!

THEN WE'LL FIGHT THEM OURSELVES!

AND BEAT THEM WITH THE AID OF THE MAGIC POTION...

...EVEN IF IT IS FATTENING!

WE DON'T NEED ANY MAGIC POTION! I SHALL GO AND SEE THESE ROMAN MATRONS. IT WILL BE EASY ENOUGH TO AGREE ON A PEACE FORMULA WOMAN TO WOMAN!

ALL THE SAME, I'D LIKE YOU TO GO AND WARN THE OTHER VILLAGE WOMEN. FOREWARNED IS FOREARMED!

WAIT A MOMENT, YOU TWO! I'VE GOT SOMETHING TO SAY TO YOU.

?

?

HOW'S MY PIGGY-WIGGY, ASTERIX? I DO HOPE HE HASN'T CAUGHT COLD!

!!!

IT'S SO DAMP IN THE FOREST AT THIS TIME OF YEAR. TAKE HIM THESE WARM CLOTHES!

AND REMIND HIM THAT IF HE OVEREATS HE'S LIABLE TO GET AN ATTACK OF THE GOUT!

FISHMONG... UN...

HERE, ASTERIX!

?

TELL UNHYGIENIX TO TO WRAP UP WELL! NIGHTS ARE CHILLY IN THE FOREST!

FOR FULLIAUTOMATIX! I KNOW THAT GREAT LOUT ...HE CATCHES COLD AT THE DROP OF A HELMET!

29a

FOR GERIATRIX, TO KEEP HIS RHEUMATICS AWAY!

AND THESE TO KEEP HIS HAND IN!

?

!

I WANT TO ASK YOU A FAVOUR, ASTERIX!

HEY, OBELIX!

HEY, ASTERIX!

OBELIX!

YOOHOO, ASTERIX!

SOON AFTERWARDS...

WELL, ASTERIX, WHAT NEWS HAVE YOU BROUGHT BACK FROM THE VILLAGE?

NOT MUCH NEWS...

...BUT NO END OF ADVICE!

?!

29b

THE CENTURY OF WOMEN HAS PITCHED TEMPORARY CAMP NEAR THE FORTIFIED CAMP OF AQUARIUM, IN LINE WITH THE REGULATIONS...

...SLIGHTLY MODIFIED HERE AND THERE!

JUST WHAT IS THIS?

THIS PRINT? IT'S A FAST DYE! GUARANTEED NOT TO RUN IN THE WASH!

SOME OF THE DISGRUNTLED MEN CONFINED TO BARRACKS NEXT DOOR RELIEVE THEIR FEELINGS ABOUT THEIR RELIEF.

IF WOMEN CAN JOIN THE LEGIONS NOW, WHAT USE ARE WE GOING TO BE?

I COULD TELL YOU! I WOULDN'T EVEN MIND BEING A *DOMESTICUS** OVER IN THAT CAMP!

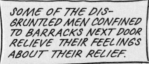

*SERVANT

MEANWHILE...

BRAVURA! SHE MUST BE GOING TO THE ROMAN CAMP! LET'S FOLLOW HER DISCREETLY!

HALT, GAUL!

YOU'RE A WOMAN TOO! THAT MAKES US SISTERS, SO LET'S SHAKES HANDS, ROMAN!

TCHAC!

THAT ROMAN SISTER ISN'T VERY GALLANT!

YOU SAID IT!

WHAT BRINGS YOU HERE, GAULISH WOMAN?

I'VE COME TO OFFER PEACE BETWEEN ROME AND THE VILLAGE OF INDOMITABLE GAULS, AND THIS IS THE WELCOME I GET!

TEEHEEHEE! SO THE INDOMITABLE GAULS ARE SURRENDERING! I WOULDN'T HAVE THOUGHT IT WOULD BE SO QUICK AND EASY!

IT'S NOT THE INDOMIT-ABLE GAULS SURRENDERING. IT'S THEIR WOMEN WHO WANT PEACE!

OH YES?

I WANT NO TRUCK WITH YOUR PEACE PROPOSALS, WOMAN! THE VILLAGE WILL BE DESTROYED, AND ITS PEOPLE WILL END THEIR DAYS IN CHAINS IN THE TULLIANUM*!

*PRISON IN ROME WHERE VERCINGETORIX AMONG OTHERS WAS INCARCERATED.

314

SMACK.

YOU'RE NOTHING BUT A LOT OF BARBARIANS!

ALL OF A SUDDEN I LIKE OUR NEW BARD BETTER!

I WANT A WORD WITH BRAVURA. SEE YOU LATER, OBELIX!

OH? RIGHT!

CONGRAT-ULATIONS ON YOUR COURAGE, BRAVURA!

HUH! JUST A SET OF OAFS! THEY'RE BENEATH OUR CONTEMPT!

YOU KNOW YOUR WAY ROUND LUTETIA, RIGHT?

I DO. WHY DO YOU ASK?

BECAUSE THIS TIME IT'S MY TURN TO MAKE YOU A PROPOSITION!

!

31 8

WE'RE AGREED, THEN, BRAVURA?

ABSOLUTELY AGREED, ASTERIX!

DONE IT! I'VE MADE MY PEACE WITH BRAVURA!

TEEHEE! SO I HEAR!

THERE GOES ANOTHER BACHELOR!

IT WAS BOUND TO HAPPEN SOME DAY!

AH, THE JOYS OF LOVE!

WHAT ARE ALL THESE SNIDE REMARKS IN AID OF?

TEE-HEEHEE!

HO,HO,HO!

YOU'VE BEEN TELLING THEM A LOAD OF NONSENSE, RIGHT?

WELL...ER...NO! YES, WELL...

I MEAN, IT'S NOTHING TO BE ASHAMED OF, ASTERIX...

OH, REALLY, YOU'RE ALL IDIOTS! I'M NOT GOING TO TELL YOU THE PLAN I'VE COOKED UP WITH BRAVURA, SO THERE!

THUD!

MEANWHILE, IN THE WOMEN LEGIONARIES' CAMP...

WELL, CENTURION, WHAT'S YOUR PLAN FOR OCCUPYING THE VILLAGE?

EASY! I BARGE IN AND I OCCUPY IT! BUT I'LL SEND A PATROL FIRST, TO BE ON THE SAFE SIDE. YOU NEVER KNOW!

YOU'RE TO GO THROUGH THE FOREST AND APPROACH THE GAULISH VILLAGE. COME BACK AND REPORT ALL YOU SEE. DISMISS!

IT STARTED WITH A HORRIBLE HOWL...

...FOLLOWED BY A DOWNPOUR WHICH BROUGHT OUT SNAKES AND SPIDERS...

...AND EVEN WOLVES!

I'M SURE THERE'S A DRAGON IN THAT FOREST!

STOP BEING SUCH DRIPS, WILL YOU?

REGULAR AS CLOCKWORK, AS PATROL FOLLOWS PATROL...

...DOWNPOUR FOLLOWS DOWNPOUR...

© OWL SWEAR-WORD

...AND DAY FOLLOWS MISERABLE DAY...

I CAN'T SEE WHY A FEW DROPS OF RAIN AND A HOWL OR SO SHOULD...

NO, WELL, YOU'RE NOT THE ONE FACING THE MUSIC, CLAPHAM-OMNIBUS!

...IN BOTH CAMPS.

THAT WAS THE LAST BOAR IN THE FOREST, AND I CAN'T EVEN COOK IT!

BLOW!

NOW, ASTERIX, ARE YOU GOING TO TELL US WHY THIS SUDDEN ENTHUSIASM FOR CACOFONIX'S SINGING?

IT'S GIVEN ME THE TIME I NEEDED TO SET UP MY PLAN!

BUT WHAT IS THIS PLAN OF YOURS?

YES, WHAT EXACTLY IS IT?

TRUST ME A LITTLE LONGER! ALL I ASK IS FOR YOU TO WAIT FOR ME NEAR THE VILLAGE, KEEPING UNDER COVER. WHATEVER HAPPENS, DON'T INTERVENE!

OBELIX AND I STILL HAVE A FEW THINGS TO DO. COMING, OBELIX?

?!

38

WHAT A SHAME! I COULD HAVE BROUGHT THE FOREST DOWN!

...AND CAESAR WILL ASK ME: 'QUID NOVI, FILI?'① AND I'LL SAY: 'VENI, VIDI, VICI!'② AND THEN HE'LL MAKE ME A SENATOR!

① WHAT NEWS, SON?
② I CAME, I SAW, I CONQUERED!

SHOW THESE GAULISH BARBARIANS THE TRUE STRENGTH OF THE ROMAN LEGIONS: THEIR ABILITY TO FIGHT WITH ORDER AND DISCIPLINE!

CHAAARGE

36ᵃ

WHEEEEEEEEEEEEEEEEEEEEEEEEEEEEEEEEEEEEEEEEEEEEEEEEEEEE

BY JUPITER, THAT'LL SHOW 'EM!

WHEEEEEEEE

WHY THIS SUDDEN SILENCE? I HOPE THE GAULS HAVE BEEN GALLANT!

36ᵇ

40

L PER C * DISCOUNT ON ALL PURCHASES!

REAL LUTETIAN LEATHER BAGS Herpes

*50% IN ROMAN NUMERALS

EEEE EE EEE!

I ORDER YOU TO...

EEEEEEEE

THIS IS A DISASTER! CAESAR WILL BE FURIOUS!

WELL DONE, ASTERIX! WHAT A GREAT PLAN!

THANKS TO BRAVURA AND ALL THE VILLAGE WOMEN, WE'VE GAULICIZED A WHOLE ROMAN LEGION!

?!?...

BOOHOO! BOOHOO!

WHAT'S THE MATTER, OBELIX?

BOOHOOOO!

I'M NO MORE USE, I'M NOT WANTED, I'M NO GOOD FOR ANYTHING!

FOLLOW ME, OBELIX! WE'RE GOING TO KEEP AN EYE ON THAT ROMAN. I'M SURE HE'S OFF TO GET HELP FROM THE FORTIFIED CAMP OF AQUARIUM. DON'T FORGET, THAT CAMP IS STILL FULL OF LEGIONARIES...
MALE LEGIONARIES!

NOT COVERED BY GAULISH GALLANTRY?

DEFINITELY NOT COVERED BY GAULISH GALLANTRY!

THEN LET'S STOP FOOLING ABOUT, ASTERIX, AND GET DOWN TO BUSINESS!

AND THE REST OF US WILL SEE TO THE OTHER CAMPS SURROUNDING THE VILLAGE! I HOPE WE WON'T RUN OUT OF MAGIC POTION?

DON'T WORRY! WE ONLY EVER RUN OUT OF A BIT OF COMMON SENSE!

WHO'S THERE?

MANLIUS CLAPHAM-OMNIBUS, ON JULIUS CAESAR'S BUSINESS!

KNOCK! KNOCK! KNOCK!

WHAT ABOUT?

THAT'S ENOUGH QUESTIONS. *I ORDER YOU TO GO AND OCCUPY THE GAULISH VILLAGE!*

BANG! BANG!

CAN'T BE DONE!

WHAT DO YOU MEAN, CAN'T BE DONE?

WE'RE CONFINED TO BARRACKS!

?!

LOOK HERE, CENTURION! THOSE COWARDLY GAULS HAVE ABANDONED THEIR VILLAGE! IT'S OCCUPIED ONLY BY THEIR WOMENFOLK, LARKING AROUND WITH THOSE ROMAN MATRONS. THIS IS YOUR CHANCE TO WIN GLORY, RICHES AND FORTUNE!

YOU... YOU MEAN IT? THERE'S NO ONE IN THE VILLAGE BUT THE WOMEN?

I SWEAR IT, BY JUPITER!

CREEAK!

SLURP!

39A

GET ARMED! GET A MOVE ON! GET TO THE GAULISH VILLAGE!

THEY'RE ALL YOURS, OBELIX!

GOODY, GOODY GOODY!

GRRRRR!

SLAM!

DON'T TOUCH ME, WHATEVER YOU DO! I AM AN ENVOY OF JULIUS CAESAR AND MAYBE WE COULD DISCUSS THE SITUATION CALMLY LIKE THE CIVILIZED FOLK WE ARE WITH A VIEW TO...

39B

TCHAC!

WE'VE GIVEN OUR DONATION!

KNOCK! KNOCK! KNOCK!

THEN FOR WHAT YOU ARE ABOUT TO RECEIVE...

CRACK!

GOOD OLD OBELIX! HE WAS FEELING RATHER LEFT OUT OF THIS ADVENTURE! I OWED HIM SOME FUN!

BING! PAF! OUCH! TCHAC! BANG!

I FEEL A LITTLE RUSTY! IT MUST BE ALL THAT RAIN-MAKING OF OUR BARD'S!

AND WE'LL SOON BE RUSTICATED!

PRETEND TO IGNORE HIM!

GRRRR!

YOU KNOW, OBELIX, I'D HAVE EXPECTED YOU TO FLATTEN THIS ROMAN CAMP COMPLETELY!

ROMAN CAMP?

AAAA...

BROOOOMMMMMMMMMCRAAAAAAAASH...

...TISHOO!

WHAT ROMAN CAMP?

LITTLE ATER...

I'M SORRY, CACOFONIX, BUT YOUR VOICE MIGHT CURDLE THE MAGIC POTION!

GLUG! GLUG!

HUH!

VILLAGERS! PROUD AND NOBLE WARRIORS! ONCE AGAIN WE FIND OURSELVES OBLIGED TO CONFRONT OUR MORTAL ENEMY! THE ANXIOUS GAZE OF THE FREE AND ANCIENT WORLD IS TURNED UPON YOUR POWERFUL BREASTS, READY TO FEND OFF THE HEGEMONY OF A DICTATORSHIP WHICH WILL GO SO FAR AS TO ATTACK WOMEN...

...AND CHILDREN!

THE GOOD POTION GUIDE SHOULD GIVE TODAY'S BREW SEVERAL STARS!

YES, AND THE ROMANS WILL SOON BE SEEING PLENTY!

CAEFAR WILL BE FURIOUF, THAT'F FOR FURE! LUCKILY WE CAN FTILL CALL ON THE OTHER FORTIFIED ROMAN CAMPF!

AND IN THE CAMP OF TOTORUM...

YOU LOOK RATHER RUFFLED, PATRICIAN! LIKE A DRINK?

YEF, PLEAFE! WITH A FTRAW IF POFFIBLE!

WELL, WELL! SO THE COWARDLY GAULS HAVE ABANDONED THEIR VILLAGE, LEAVING ONLY WOMEN AND CHILDREN TO GUARD IT!

JUFT AF I FAID, FENTURION! SLUP!

RAISE THE ALARM! THE GAULS ARE ATTACKING!!!

?!

CHARGE, BOYS!

LEAVE THEM TO ME! LEAVE THEM TO ME!

DON'T BE SELFISH, OBELIX!

CRAAÂSH!!

PUFF!

PANT!

GASP!

I FEEL MY MORALE RISING, ASTERIX!

YOU SEE, IT DIDN'T TAKE MUCH!

GOING TO BE OKAY, FENTURION?

YEF, BUT ONLY WITH A FTRAW!

42

IN BOTH THE CAMP OF LAUDANUM...

RAISE THE ALARM! THE GAULS ARE...

CRAAAASH!!

PUFF! PUFF! IF THIS GOES ON I'M DROPPING OUT! PUFF! GASP!

...AND THE CAMP OF COMPENDIUM, THE GAULISH ATTACK TAKES THE ROMANS ENTIRELY BY SURPRISE!

IN MY VIEW THE GAULS TOOK US ENTIRELY BY SURPRISE, CENTURION!

IDIOT! I NEED A PICK-ME-UP... WITH A FTRAW!

42

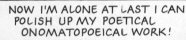

HERE, PIGGYWIGGY! THE SHIELD SUITS YOU BETTER THAN ME!

YOU KNOW YOU CAN USE IT WHENEVER YOU LIKE,'PEDI... 'PEDIMENTA!

NO HARD FEELINGS, BRAVURA?

NO HARD FEELINGS, ASTERIX!

ALL'S WELL THAT ENDS WELL. A CERTAIN CHEERFULNESS EVEN SEEMS TO HAVE CREPT INTO ROME... OR MOST OF IT!

THERE'S A STRANGE SENSE OF GAIETY IN ROME, O CAESAR!

SHUT UP, IDIOT, AND PACK MY BAGS! I'M GOING AWAY TO MY COUNTRY PALACE FOR A WHILE!

HA! HA! HA! HEE! HEE! HEE! HEE! HO! HO! HO! HO! HO! HO! HEE! HEE! HEE! HA! HA! HO! HO! HO! HEE! HEE! HA! HA! HA!

AND FINALLY, IN HAPPY CELEBRATION OF THE RETURN OF DOMESTIC PEACE AND GENERAL GOODWILL, THE TRADITIONAL BANQUET IS HELD IN THE MIDDLE OF THE VILLAGE. BRAVURA AND ALL THE GAULISH WOMEN ARE GUESTS OF HONOUR. EVEN CACOFONIX IS INVITED... ON CERTAIN CONDITIONS.

FRIENDS, GAULS, COUNTRYMEN! IT IS WITH DEEP EMOTION THAT...

DO YOU LIKE IT IN OUR VILLAGE, BRAVURA?

YES, BUT I MUST GET BACK TO LUTETIA SOON! AND BY WAY OF APOLOGY I'VE PROMISED TO TAKE YOUR BARD BACK WITH ME AND INTRODUCE HIM TO ZIEGFELDFOLLIX, THE GREAT LUTETIAN IMPRESARIO!

SCRUNCH! SCRUNCH!

I JUTHT CAN'T WAIT TO BE GROWN UP AND HAVE FUN!

ME TOO! THEN I'LL BE YOUR CHIEF!

The End

UDERZO-91